Made in the USA
Las Vegas, NV
15 March 2023

69125615R00061